NOTE ON PHOTOGRAPHS

Two very different kinds of photos were selected for WHERE DO HORSES LIVE. One set was taken in Montana and Wyoming. It includes images of horse country, horses on large ranches, and photos of truly wild horses that still roam free. These wild horses are descendants of the first horses brought to North America by explorers, horses that escaped from early day ranchers, and horses that once belonged to the Crow people and other native Americans. Fortunately, some wild horses now live on preserves established to protect these magnificent animals. You can see wild horses at Pryor Mountain Wild Horse Range on the border of Wyoming and Montana. And you can learn more about wild horses by reading Hope Ryden's fascinating book, AMERICA'S LAST WILD HORSES.

The other set of photographs were taken at horse shows, rodeos, stables, and other places where people and horses live together in Washington State. We hope this introduction is enjoyed by all who own a horse or dream that wonderful dream.

and where horse and rider share a home.

They live by themselves

and where crowds of people cheer.

Horses live where best
friends gather

and wherever cowboys ride
the cattle trail.

in barns on quiet country roads,

Horses live in stables where the city fills the sky.

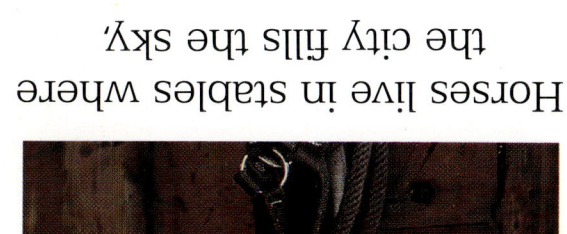

and on the open plain.

beside the sea,

high in western mountains,

and where they watch their
newborns grow.

winter snow,

Horses live in fresh spring grass,

For Bren, her pony, and her big sky dreams . . .   R.H.

Copyright © 1989 by Ron Hirschi and Linda Quartman Younker

All rights reserved. No part of this book may be reproduced or
transmitted in any form or by any means, electronic or mechanical,
including photocopying, recording, or by any information storage
and retrieval system, without permission in writing from the
Publisher.

First published in the United States of America in 1989
by Walker Publishing Company, Inc.

Published simultaneously in Canada by Thomas Allen & Son
Canada, Limited, Markham, Ontario

Library of Congress Cataloging-in-Publication Data

Hirschi, Ron.
Where do horses live? / Ron Hirschi ; photographs by Linda Younker.
p.   cm.
Summary: Brief text and photographs present the places where
both wild and domestic horses live.
ISBN 0-8027-6878-4.—ISBN 0-8027-6879-2 (lib. bdg.)
1. Horses—Juvenile literature. [1. Horses.] I. Younker, Linda,
ill. II. Title.
SF302.H58   1989   88-36649
636.1'0831—dc19   CIP   AC

Printed in Hong Kong

10   9   8   7   6   5   4   3   2   1

WHERE DO HORSES LIVE?

Ron Hirschi

photographs by
Linda Quartman Younker and **Ron Hirschi**

Walker and Company
New York